DIRECT MAIL

ROCKPORT
PUBLISHERS

Rockport Publishers, Inc.
Rockport, Massachusetts

First published in the United States of America by:
Rockport Publishers, Inc.
146 Granite Street
Rockport, Massachusetts 01966-1299
Telephone: (508) 546-9590
Fax: (508) 546-7141

Distributed to the trade by:
Consortium Book Sales & Distribution, Inc.
1045 Westgate Drive
Saint Paul, MN 55114
(612) 221-9035
(800) 283-3572

Other Distribution by:
Rockport Publishers, Inc.
Rockport, Massachusetts 01966-1299

ISBN 1-56496-337-3

10 9 8 7 6 5 4 3 2 1

Layout: Sara Day Graphic Design
Cover Images: *clockwise from top left:*
Hornall Anderson Design Works,
Janet Hughes and Associates,
Love Packaging Group,
Siebert Design Associates,
The Weller Institute for the Cure of Design,
SullivanPerkins

Manufactured in Hong Kong by Regent Publishing Services Limited

INTRODUCTION

When a company sends an eye-catching direct-mail piece appropriate to its mailing list, great things happen. New clients call. Old subscribers renew. Contestants enter sweepstakes. Investors invest. What are the graphic design tricks that make a letter stand out in a box full of junk mail?

Design Library: Direct Mail shows the best pieces published by Rockport in its renowned collections of graphic design. Each direct-mail design shows creative use of color, and excellent, effective solutions to budget and size constraints. This anthology not only serves as a record of the work of cutting-edge design firms, but also will inspire new designs from up-and-coming commercial artists.

The honeycomb used in this piece is an inexpensive addition that supports the graphic and makes the brochure memorable.

Design Firm: Graef & Ziller Design
Art Directors: Barbara Ziller, Andrew Graef
Designers: Barbara Ziller, Andrew Graef
Illustrator: Elaine Hodges
Copywriter: Andrew Graef
Client: Graef & Ziller Design
Paper/Printer: Evergreen, Linotext GTO (Heidelberg Digital Press)
Tools: QuarkXPress, Adobe Illustrator, Adobe Photoshop

Design Firm: Leo in House
Art Director: Karsten Lentge
Copywriters: Karsten Lentge, Preben Schroder
Client: Leo Pharmaceutical
Paper: Royal Consort, Silk
Tool: QuarkXPress

Design Firm: Sayles Graphic Design
Art Director: John Sayles
Designer: John Sayles
Illustrator: John Sayles
Copywriter: Wendy Lyons
Client: Cutler Travel Marketing
Paper/Printer: Curtis Paper, Artcraft Printing,
The Printing Station

Printed on text weight paper to save costs, the introductory brochure mails in a glassine envelope. The corporate brochure is a three-dimensional encounter—with foreign coins and stamps, postcards, maps, and travel memorabilia from around the globe, attached by hand to its multicolored pages.

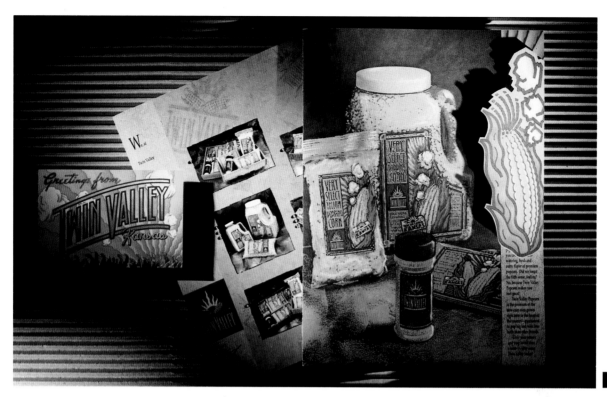

1

2

3

1 This Twin Valley Popcorn promotional package is sent to consumers and retailers. It includes a postcard, general info folder, and catalog sheet with an order form.

Design Firm: Love Packaging Group
Art Director/Designer: Tracy Holdeman
Illustrator: Tracy Holdeman
Client: Twin Valley Popcorn

2 "This is not a foreign language," states this mailer for an auto repair shop that wanted to promote the addition of Asian makes to its list of cars serviced. "The client resisted the tendency to include a lot of copy," notes Sayles. "It's short, to the point, and it worked."

Design Firm: Sayles Graphic Design
Art Director/Designer: John Sayles
Illustrator: John Sayles
Client: Beckley Imports

3 A newly formed digital type foundry, established by designer Carlos Segura, promoted its fonts by sending off a variety of promotional items in an intriguing drawstring bag. "This promotion literally put us on the map," says Segura.

Design Firm: Segura, Inc.
Art Director/Designer:
Carlos Segura
Client: T-26

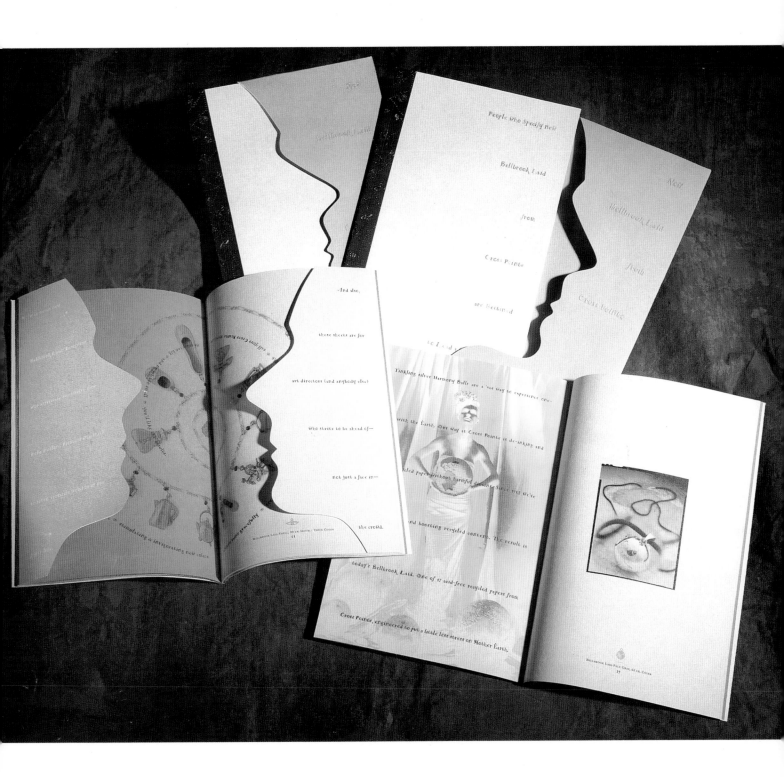

Showing off the printing capabilities of text with a laid finish meant pushing the limits of the stock. "This piece extended traditional perceptions of how a laid finish stock performs," says Little & Company art director Mike Lizama.

Design Firm: Little & Company
Art Director/Designer: Mike Lizama
Client: Cross Pointe Paper Corp.

If one advances confidently in the direction of his dreams,
and endeavors to live the life that he has imagined,
he will meet with a success unexpected in common hours.

-- *Henry David Thoreau*

Designed and printed by Karen & Bruce Licher at
INDEPENDENT PROJECT PRESS

R.E.M.

Post Office Box 8032

ATHENS, GA.
30603

BULK RATE
U.S. POSTAGE
PAID
ATHENS
GEORGIA
PERMIT NO.
438

R.E.M. Christmas Card & Holiday Stayflat

Design Firm: Independent Project Press
Art Director/Designers: Karen & Bruce Licher
Illustrator: Karen Licher
Client: R.E.M./Athens, Ltd.

THE COMMUNITY CHEST
OF HONG KONG
TWENTY SECOND
ANNUAL REPORT 1990/91
香港公益金第二十二期年報
一九九〇至九一年度

爲善最樂・福有攸歸

The Community Chest of Hong Kong
Twenty-Second Annual Report

The center image on the work is a Chinese New
Year motif meaning "happiness." The Chinese
character is made up of objects and photographs relevant to each of the services men-
tioned in the brochure. The entire piece is
printed on recycled paper.

Design Firm: Kan Tài-keung Design &
Associates, Ltd.
Art Director: Kan Tài-keung/Eddy Yu Chi Kong
Designer: Eddy Yu Chi Kong/Joyce Hó Ngai Sing
Photographer: Franklin Lau
Client: The Community Chest of Hong Kong

Designer: Renée Kremer and Kimberly Cooke
Photographer: Mark C. Hartley/Jon Durant
Copywriter: Kimberly Cooke
Client: Visual Arts Alliance
Printing: 5-color PMS, Karma, UV Ultra Wrapper

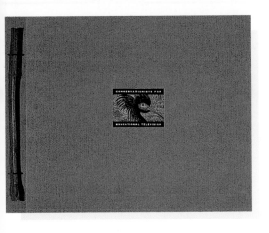

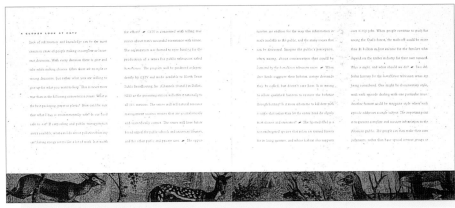

1 Features multiple die-cuts and a small brochure adhered to the end panel.

Design Firm: Sayles Graphic Design
Art Director: John Sayles
Designer: John Sayles
Illustrator: John Sayles
Copywriter: LuAnn Harkins
Client: Associates General Contractors
Printing: 3-color on Chipboard Astrobrite Kraft Paper and Chipboard

2
Design Firm: SullivanPerkins
Art Director: Ron Sullivan
Designer: Dan Richards
Illustrator: Dan Richards
Copywriter: CETV
Client: Conservationists for Educational Television
Printing: 2-color on Champion Benefit, bound with a twig

This piece reintroduced a paper that had been improved and updated with a more contemporary color palette. It includes extensive production notes for its audience of designers and printers. "It was intended to be an idea generator, but also an educational tool," says Paul Wharton of Little & Company.

Design Firm: Little & Company
Art Director/Designer: Mike Lizama
Copywriter: Sandra Bucholtz
Client: Cross Pointe Paper Corp.

(facing page)

Showcasing this printer's capability required a multicomponent mailer that included a poster, an indentifier and gift card. The mailing was sent to current and potential clients.

Design Firm: Janet Hughes and Associates
Art Director/Designer: Donna Perzel
Photographer: Stephen Hone
Calligrapher: Paul DeCampli
Client: Phototype Color Graphics

Mann's Diamond Buyers Brochure

All artwork for this brochure was pre-existing. The two-color design, printed on colored paper for a multicolored effect, is accentuated in color and texture by a "trash" stock paper.

Design Firm: Muller + Company Guide
All Design: Jon Simonsen

Barnard Annual Funds Brochure

The text and architectural photographs were printed 1-color for a very inexpensive press run. These pieces are designed to fit into Barnard's existing envelopes for cost-effective mailing.

Design Firm: Platinum Design, Inc.
Designer: Ara Schlesinger
Art Director: Ara Schlesinger
Photographer: Paul LachenAuer

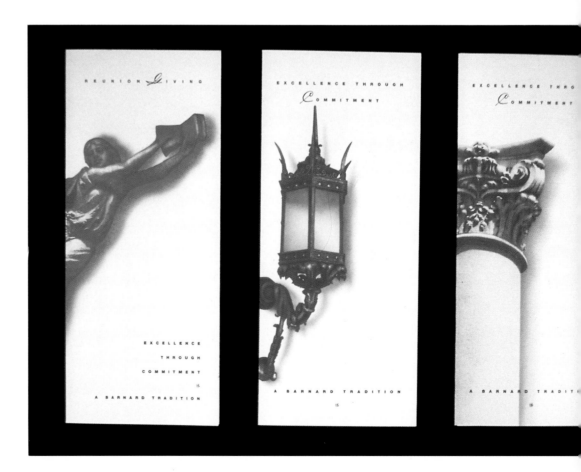

Guild Brochure

Production budget could only afford one printing color, so the paper color, reverses, and interesting ink color were chosen to achieve a range of colors.

Design Firm: Planet Design Company
All Design: Dana Lytle

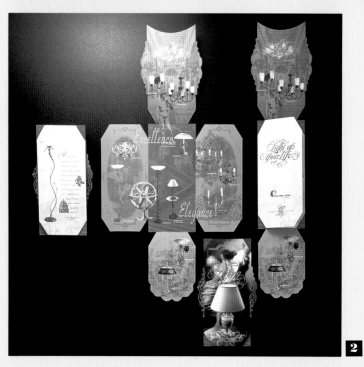

1
Design Firm: Segura Inc.
Art Director: Carlos Segura
Designer: Carlos Segura
Client: Segura Inc.
Printer: Argus Press
Tools: Adobe Illustrator, QuarkXPress, and Adobe Photoshop

2 This piece was created entirely by hand.

Design Firm: Grand Design Co.
Art Directors: Grand So, Kwong Chi Man
Designer: Kwong Chi Man
Illustrator: Kwong Chi Man
Photographer: David Lo
Client: Hop Shing Loong Lighting Ltd.
Printer: Reliance Production

Used as a follow-up piece for résumés, this brochure was photocopied in-house to save costs, then assembled by hand.

Design Firm: Shari Flack
Art Director: Shari Flack
Designer: Shari Flack
Copywriter: Shari Flack
Client: Shari Flack
Paper: Arvey
Tool: QuarkXPress

17

The "thank-you bag" is included as a gift to the recipient for requesting the kit.

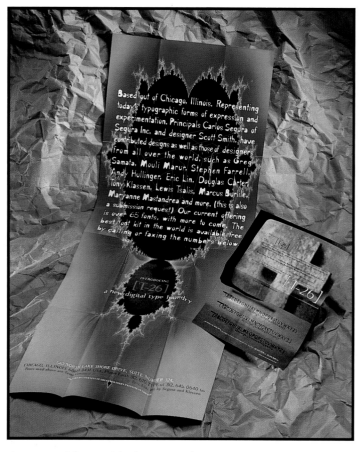

A poster and flyer explain the company's mission and solicit font contributors. Artwork from the poster was also used as a magazine ad to promote [T-26].

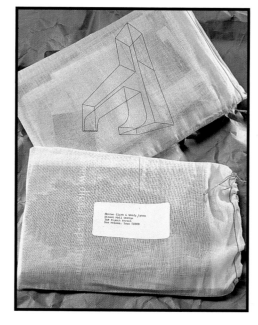

The [T-26] mailing is made from recycled materials and found objects. Contents of the kits change constantly— 10 have been produced so far—and are quickly becoming collectible.

The font catalog is unbound so it can be updated daily on a computer.

Client: [T-26]
Design Firm: Segura, Inc., Chicago, Illinois
Art Director: Carlos Segura
Designer: Carlos Segura, Scott Smith
Copywriter: Dan X. O'Neil

sing "In/Out" as a theme, this mailing is part of a campaign for a ommunications competition. Winning entrants receive a preview vitation and a kraft liquor bag to bring to the BYOB event.

lient: Dallas Society of Visual Communications
esign Firm: Sibley/Peteet Design, Inc., Dallas, Texas
rt Director: Rex Peteet
esigner: Rex Peteet, Derek Welch
lustrator: Rex Peteet, Derek Welch, Mike Schroeder
hotographer: Phil Hollenbeck

Individual vellum sheets differentiate each product line in this eyewear collection. Joined by a paper strap, the mailing can be modified according to specific needs.

Client: eyeOTA
Design Firm: Wilshire Design, Culver City, California
Art Director: David Kilvert
Designer: Krista Kilvert, David Kilvert

This series of mailings promotes a line of ready-to-wear accessories. High-action photography and close-up shots add youthful appeal.

Client: 1x1:z (Japan)
Design FIrm: Sam Smidt Studio, Palo Alto, California
All Design By: Sam Smidt
Photographer: Raja Muna

Design Firm: Sayles Graphic Design
Art Director: John Sayles
Designer: John Sayles
Occasion: Wedding
Illustrator: John Sayles
Client: The Blumenthal Family

Alice, Larry and Richie, parrot Harry Bird, and cats Russie Mae Douglas, Team D.J. Spootwater, Dasser Buckles, and Miss Kitty have moved (but not the home, of course). You can now find them at 11306 Silvermoon Row, Columbia, Maryland 21044.

1
Design Firm: SullivanPerkins
Art Director: Art Garcia
Designer: Art Garcia
Occasion: Moving Announcement
Illustrator: Art Garcia
Client: Wolf Family

2
Design Firm: Mires Design, Inc.
Art Director: Scott Mires
Designer: Scott Mires
Occasion: Moving Announcement
Photographer: Chris Wimpey
Client: Mires Design, Inc.

A 5" x 5" x 5" box attracts attention—the die-cut brochure inside keeps it. The project uses only two colors of ink.

Client: Crowley Mandelbaum
Design Firm: Sayles Graphic Design, Des Moines, Iowa
All Design By: John Sayles
Photographer: Jim Cobb

To introduce a new product—the Pinnacle bottle—the distributor sent out sample bottles to purchasing agents.

Client: Berlin Packaging
Design Firm: Sayles Graphic Design, Des Moines, Iowa
All Design By: John Sayles

A holiday card for a Hong Kong design organization, this design wishes recipients both "Merry Christmas" and "Happy Chinese New Year" with an interchangeable visual suited to both greetings.

Client: PPA Design
Design Firm: PPA Design, Hong Kong
All Design By: Byron Jacobs

This campaign promotes a popcorn company with postcards, catalog sheets, and a coordinating folder.

Client: Twin Valley Popcorn
Design Firm: Love Packaging Group, Wichita, Kansas
All Design By: Tracy Holdeman
Photographer: Rock Island Studios

By using a Z-fold, this mailer actually has two covers: one on each side.

Client: Bradley Printing
Design Firm: Liska and Associates, Inc., Chicago, Illinois
Art Director: Steven Liska
photographer: Scott Morgan

Only seven hundred of these unique promotions were produced by the design firm. Each was individually numbered.

Client: Concrete
Design Firm: Concrete, Chicago, Illinois
Art Director: Jilly Simons
Designer: Jilly Simons, David Robson
Images: Geof Kern
Words: Deborah Barron

LEO BURNETT HAS MOVED TO 6th FLOOR CITYPLAZA 3. 14 TAIKOO WAN RD. HONG KONG. TEL: 567 4333 FAX: 885 3209

Leo Burnett Moves, Moving Card

For this card, the use of a photographer's assistant as a model avoided all model fees. No background creation or set up was required either.

Design Firm: The Design Group
Designer: Stefan Sagmeister, Peter Rae
Art Director: Stefan Sagmeister
Photographer: Arthur Schulten

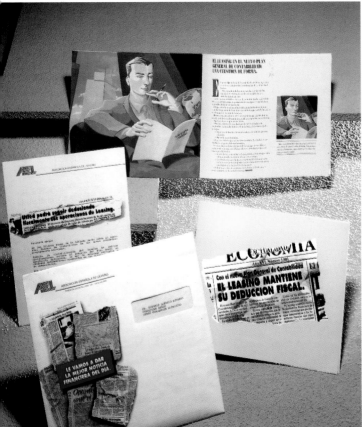

Asociación Española de Leasing

The design for this mailing used pre-existing images and logos to stay within the budget. The mailing format proved more cost-efficient than a traditional general campaign.

Design Firm: Rapp Collins Communications
Designer: Javier Arcos Pitarque
Art Director: Javier Arcos Pitarque

Rennies Catalogue

This mail order catalogue for an antique dealer was printed in black-and-white. A wraparound dust jacket was made from an existing pattern paper with an applied label. The job was labor-intensive but the materials were inexpensive.

Design Firm: Trickett & Webb
All Design: Lynn Trickett, Brian Webb

Mailing Advertisement

This launch brochure was printed 2-color to eliminate high printing costs.

Design Firm: Trickett & Webb
Designer: Steve Edwards
Art Director: Lynn Trickett, Brian Webb

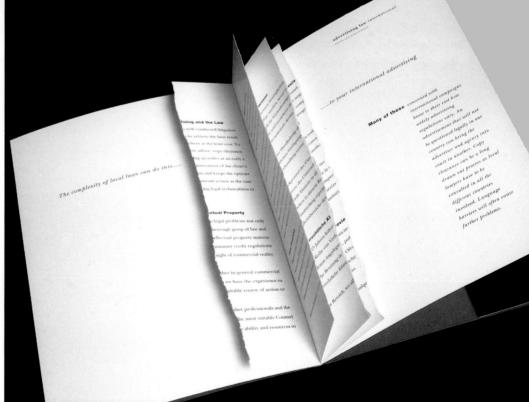

1
Design Firm: Siebert Design Associates
Art Director: Lori Siebert
Designer: Lori Siebert
Occasion: Family Day Museum Opening
Illustrator: Lori Siebert
Client: Cincinnati Art Museum

2
Design Firm: WS Design
Art Director: Wayne Sakamoto
Designer: Wayne Sakamoto
Occasion: Re-Opening Celebration
Client: Tamalpais Dog Grooming

BIG DEALS

BIG DAY. Thursday, November 5, during this year's ICSC Deal Making Convention in Dallas, Gary Shafer and the retail partners of Trammell Crow Company invite you to a special after-hours party. It's a great way to end a big day.

BIG TIME. That evening from 7:30 P.M. to 10:30 P.M. we'll host a buffet and cocktails. Transportation to the party will be provided from the Anatole Hotel, Chantilly Entrance, at 7:15, 7:30 and 7:45 P.M., with return service every fifteen minutes. So make plans to have a great time with us.

Design Firm: SullivanPerkins
Art Director: Ron Sullivan
Designer: Michael Sprong
Occasion: Building Opening
Illustrator: Michael Sprong
Client: Trammel Crow Company

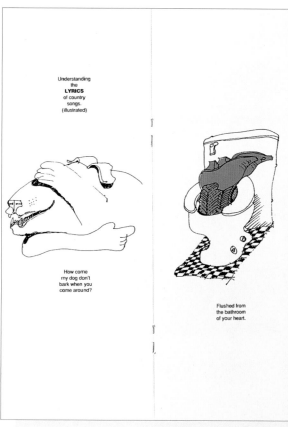

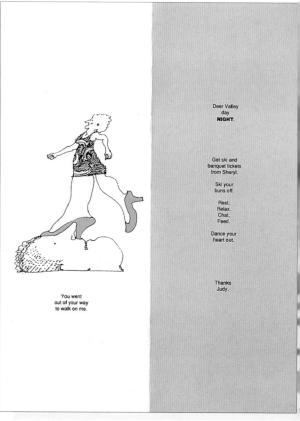

Design Firm: The Weller Institute for the
Cure of Design
Art Director: Don Weller
Designer: Don Weller
Illustrator: Don Weller
Client: The Design Conference That Just
Happens To Be In Park City, UT 1994
Printing: 2-color, Lustro Dull Cover

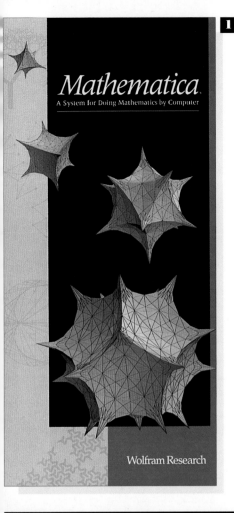

Mathematica.
A System for Doing Mathematics by Computer

Wolfram Research

科学技術計算のための決定的システム

Mathematica.

Wolfram Research

1 All graphics images created with
Mathematica.

Design Firm: Wolfram Research
Publications Dept.
Art Director:
John Bonadies
Designer: John Bonadies
Copywriter: Joe Grohens
Client: Wolfram Research, Inc.
Printing: 6-color on Paralux

2 All graphics images created with
Mathematica. Japanese text created with
Adobe Kanji PageMaker.

Design Firm: Wolfram Research
Publications Dept.
Art Director: John Bonadies
Designer: Jody Jasinski
Copywriter: Joe Grohen/Caron Allen
Client: Wolfram Research, Inc.
Printing: 5-color on Warren Recovery Gloss

3
Design Firm: Sommese Design
Art Director: Lanny Sommese
Designer: Brian Hatcher
Illustrator: Lanny Sommese
Copywriter: Katherine Talcott
Client: Central Pennsylvania Festival of the Arts
Printing: 1-color on Cross-Pointe Genesis
(Recycled)

For this fraternity/sorority "rush" recruitment mailing, the designer used found objects, including paper remnants from a recently completed corporate project, scrap corrugated cardboard, and industrial office supply materials. Perhaps the most innovative material found is the front cover of the piece; it is an actual metal printing plate. Although they were never actually used in the printing process, the plates have been burned with the project title "Greek Life: Get A Feel For It."

Design Firm: Sayles Graphic Design
Art Director: John Sayles
Designer: John Sayles
Illustrator: John Sayles
Copywriter: Wendy Lyons
Client: Drake University
Paper/Printer: Curtis Tuscan Antique, Action Print, Acme Printing

This brochure comes in a box with a real banana and plum. Two thousand pieces were sent out during a summer heat wave, making production a nightmare. The bananas were rotten by the time the plums arrived, but in the end, the project was a success. Most of the packages were hand-delivered.

Design Firm: M & Company
Art Director: Stefan Sagmeister
Designer: Stefan Sagmeister and Tom Walker
Illustrator: Tom Walker
Copywriters: Lee Brown and Stefan Sagmeister
Client: Gay and Lesbian Task Force
Paper/Printer: 80 lb. uncoated corrugated box, tissue paper

Beautiful images, shot both in-studio and on location, form the basis for this sensitive promotion for a photographer.

Client: Craig Cutler Studio
Design Firm: Wood Design, New York, New York
Art Director: Tom Wood
Designer: Tom Wood
Photographer: Craig Cutler

Designed to resemble a dictionary, this mailer concludes with a pop-up business reply card. Only one color of ink was used to produce the piece.

Client: MWR Telecom
Design Firm: Sayles Graphic Design, Des Moines, Iowa
All Design By: John Sayles
Photographer: Bill Nellans

An elegant promotion for an office building campus, this wire-bound booklet is unique in its use of typography and duotone photographs.

Client: Louis Dreyfus Property Group
Design Firm: Wood Design, New York, New York
All Design By: Tom Wood

David Carter Design Associates' holiday greeting was mailed in a simple corrugated box. A paper belly-band and mailing label containing holiday images hint at what's inside.

Each card depicts a different country's holiday through visuals and copy explaining the celebration and a traditional recipe.

The recipe box was mailed to David Carter Design Associates' clients throughout the world. Locally, it also served as an invitation to the firm's holiday party.

Client/Design Firm: David Carter Design Associates, Dallas, Texas
Art Directors: David Carter, Lori B. Wilson, Sharon LeJeune
Designer: Sharon LeJeune
Copy Editor: Bill Baldwin
Illustrators: Michael Crampton, Lynn Rowe Read, Connie Connally, Rick Smith
Photographers:
Grace Knott, Dick Patrick, Neal Farris, Ben Britt

Design: Design: M/W
Art Director: Allison Muench, J.P. Williams
Occasion: Opening Announcement
Client: Takashimaya New York

Design Firm: Studio MD
Art Director: Jesse Doquilo, Randy Lim,
Glenn Mitsui
Designer: Jesse Doquilo
Occasion: Moving Announcement
Photographer: Jesse Doquilo
Illustrator: Jesse Doquilo
Client: Studio MD

This brochure promotes an annual fundraiser with travel as its theme. Its designer, Lana Rigsby, used rare stamps borrowed from a local collector as a visual theme. Rigsby says the piece drew a large crowd: "Attendance was up 20 percent over the prior year," she reports.

Design Firm: Rigsby Design, Inc.
Art Director/Designer: Lana Rigsby
Illustrator: Lana Rigsby, Deborah Brochstein
Client: Alley Theatre, Houston

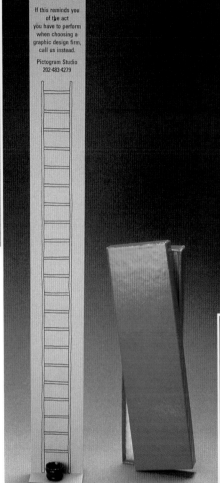

Each of the boxes in this promotional series was sent to a prospective client every two to three weeks. "They've really helped us break the ice with new clients," says firm principal Stephanie Hooton.

Design Firm: Pictogram Studio
Art Director: Hien Nguyen
Designer: Hien Nguyen, Stephanie Hooton
Client: Pictogram Studio

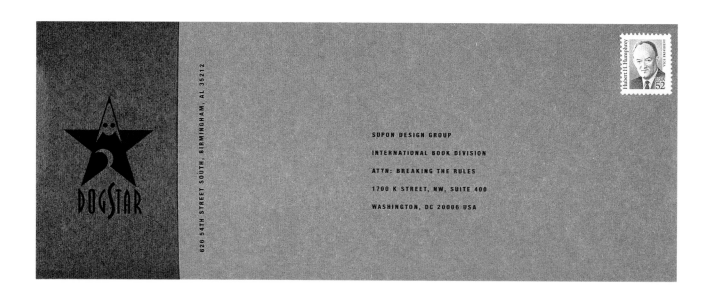

Objective: To create a self-promotion that reflects the designer's illustration and design skills, as well as "a view of the world" from his corner.

Innovation: Construction paper printed through a laser printer gives this handmade piece its unique composition. This promotion features Davidson's best logos and an entertaining group of true and folksy stories to accompany them and provide insight into his design process.

Design Firm: Dogstar Design
Art Director: Rodney Davidson
Designer: Rodney Davidson
Illustrator: Rodney Davidson
Copywriter: Rodney Davidson
Client: Dogstar Design

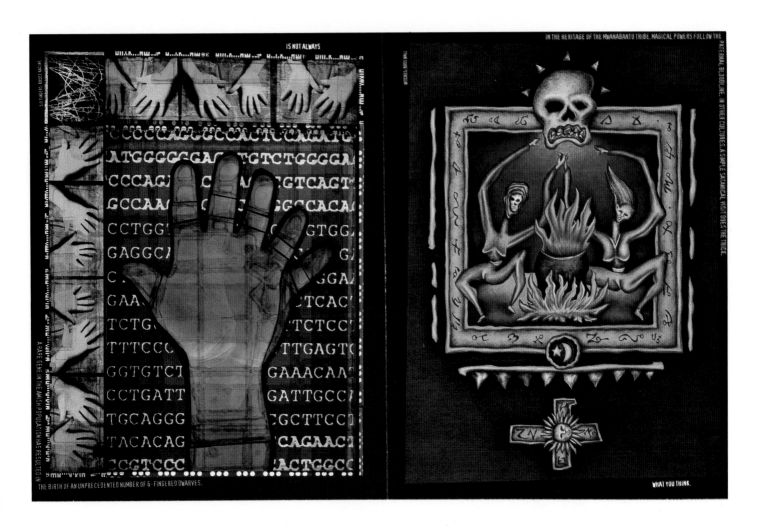

Objective: To demonstrate to the design community the client's ability to deliver top-quality printing.

Innovation: Instead of the typical listing of equipment available and clients served, unusual typography and a slightly deranged play on the meaning of the word "heritage" help set this printer's advertisement apart from its competitors. The insert also opens backwards—on the left side rather than the right.

Design Firm: After Hours Creative
Art Director: Russ Haan
Designer: Todd Fedell
Illustrators: Rose Johnson, Bruce Racine, Russ Wall, Brian Marsland
Client: Heritage Graphics

Everyone who receives a box will open it. This one was also hand addressed and therefore very appealing.

Client: Helene Curtis/Golin Harris
Design Firm: Steve Meek Incorporated, Chicago, Illinois
All Design By: Steve Meek

This invitation promotes the grand opening of the National Postal Museum at the Smithsonian Institution in Washington, D.C. The oversized piece is mailed out in the same glassine envelopes the Postal Service uses to hold sheets of stamps.

Client: Hines Interests Limited Partnership
Design Firm: Rigsby Design, Inc., Houston, Texas
Art Director: Lana Rigsby
Designer: Lana Rigsby, Michael B. Thede

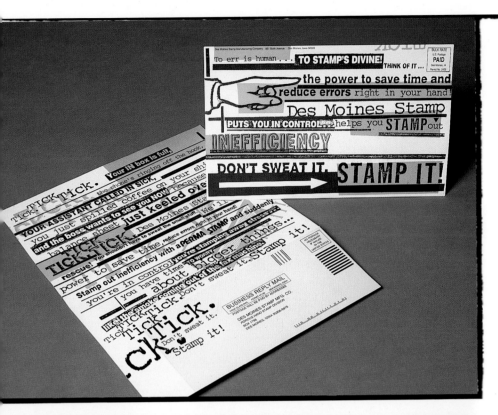

In the slick and glossy mail marketplace, this rough-edged postcard mailer makes a statement.

Client: Des Moines Stamp Manufacturing
Design Firm: Sayles Graphic Design, Des Moines, Iowa
All Design By: John Sayles

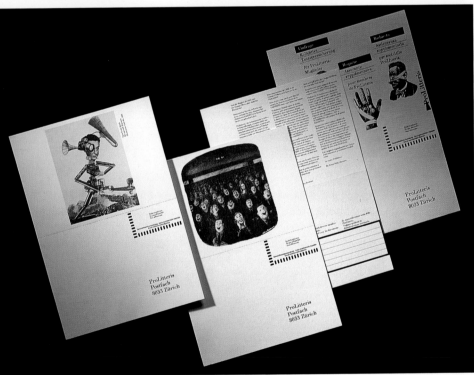

This simple and straightforward series of direct-mail pieces is recruiting more ProLitteris members. Target audience: Writers, journalists, authors, artists, and graphic designers.

Client: ProLitteris
Design Firm: Gottschalk & Ash International, Zürich, Switzerland
Designer: Fritz Gottschalk, Andreas Gossweiler
Illustrator: Chas Addams, Otto Umbehr

1

2

1
Design Firm: Studio MD
Art Director: Carol Phillips,
Maritz Performance
Improvement Co.
Designer: Jesse Doquilo,
Studio MD
Occasion: Nissan Dealer
Announcement Show
Illustrator: Jesse Doquilo
Client: Nissan

2
Design Firm: SullivanPerkins
Art Director: Ron Sullivan
Designer: Jon Flaming
Occasion: Merchants
Renovation Announcement
Illustrator: Jon Flaming
Client: Topanga Plaza/
Centermark Development

(facing page)
Design Firm: Siebert Design
Associates
Art Director: Lori Siebert
Designer: Lori Siebert,
Jeff Fassnacht
Occasion: Fundraiser
Illustrator: John Patrick
Client: School for Creative
& Performing Arts

Trust and the School for Creative and Performing Arts present

Tickets
632-5910

ov.
-29

OLiVeR!

The Taft Th

SCPA

The 1

THE FRIENDS OF THE SCHOOL FOR
CREATIVE AND PERFORMING ARTS
1310 Sycamore Street
Cincinnati, Ohio 45210

NON-PROFIT ORG.
U.S. POSTAGE
PAID
PERMIT NO. 4388
CINCINNATI, OHIO

ordially Invite Y

Gala Committee Members

The SCPA production of "Oliver!" is sponsored by Central Trust

5:30 pm.

"Consider Yourself"
part of the London
scene, enjoying
cocktails and hors
d'oeuvres while
surrounded by
strolling musicians.

6:45 pm.

Feast on "Food,
Glorious Food" (no
gruel here!) at a
sumptuous four
course dinner, while
overlooking the
London Bridge.

8:30 pm.

As Big Ben chimes,
the curtain will
rise on the SCPA
production

Gala
Atrium II
221 East Fourth Street

OLiVeR!
with a Twist

honors SCPA's own
Dianne Dunkelman.

"She'd Do Anything"
for us and we
consider ourselves
lucky that she's "Part
of the Family."

Taft Theatre
Production
5th & Sycamore

ordially Invite Y

he Christmas season has spe-
al meaning for the different
embers of Samata Associates'
am. This holiday promotion
ves each staffer an opportu-
ty to share their seasonal
ntiments.

esign Firm: Samata Associates
t Director: Pat Samata
esigners: Pat Samata,
reg Samata
hotographer: Jean Moss
ustrator: George Sawa
lient: Samata Associates

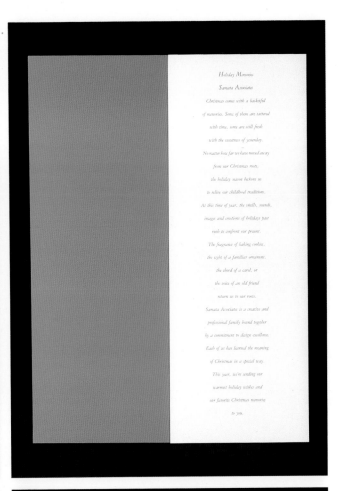

Holiday Memories
Samata Associates

Christmas comes with a basketful
of memories. Some of them are tattered
with time, some are still fresh
with the sweetness of yesterday.
No matter how far we have moved away
from our Christmas roots,
the holiday season beckons us
to relive our childhood traditions.
At this time of year, the smells, sounds,
images and emotions of holidays past
rush to confront our present.
The fragrance of baking cookies,
the sight of a familiar ornament,
the chord of a carol, or
the voice of an old friend
return us to our roots.
Samata Associates is a creative and
professional family bound together
by a commitment to design excellence.
Each of us has learned the meaning
of Christmas in a special way.
This year, we're sending our
warmest holiday wishes and
our favorite Christmas memories
to you.

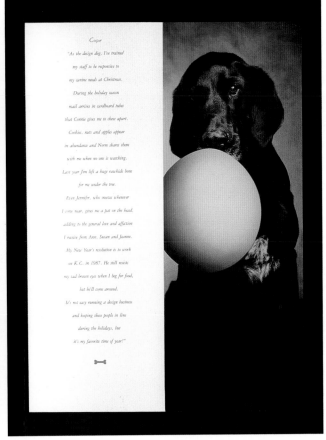

(facing page)
This series of six oversized postcards was conceived
to promote a variety of design approaches. They
were mailed over a two-month period. "My follow-
up calls immediately indicated a positive response
to the mailings," says Monderer.

Design Firm: Stewart Monderer Design, Inc.
Art Director: Stewart Monderer
Designers: Robert Davison, Jane Winsor
Illustrator: Richard Goldberg
Client: Stewart Monderer Design, Inc.

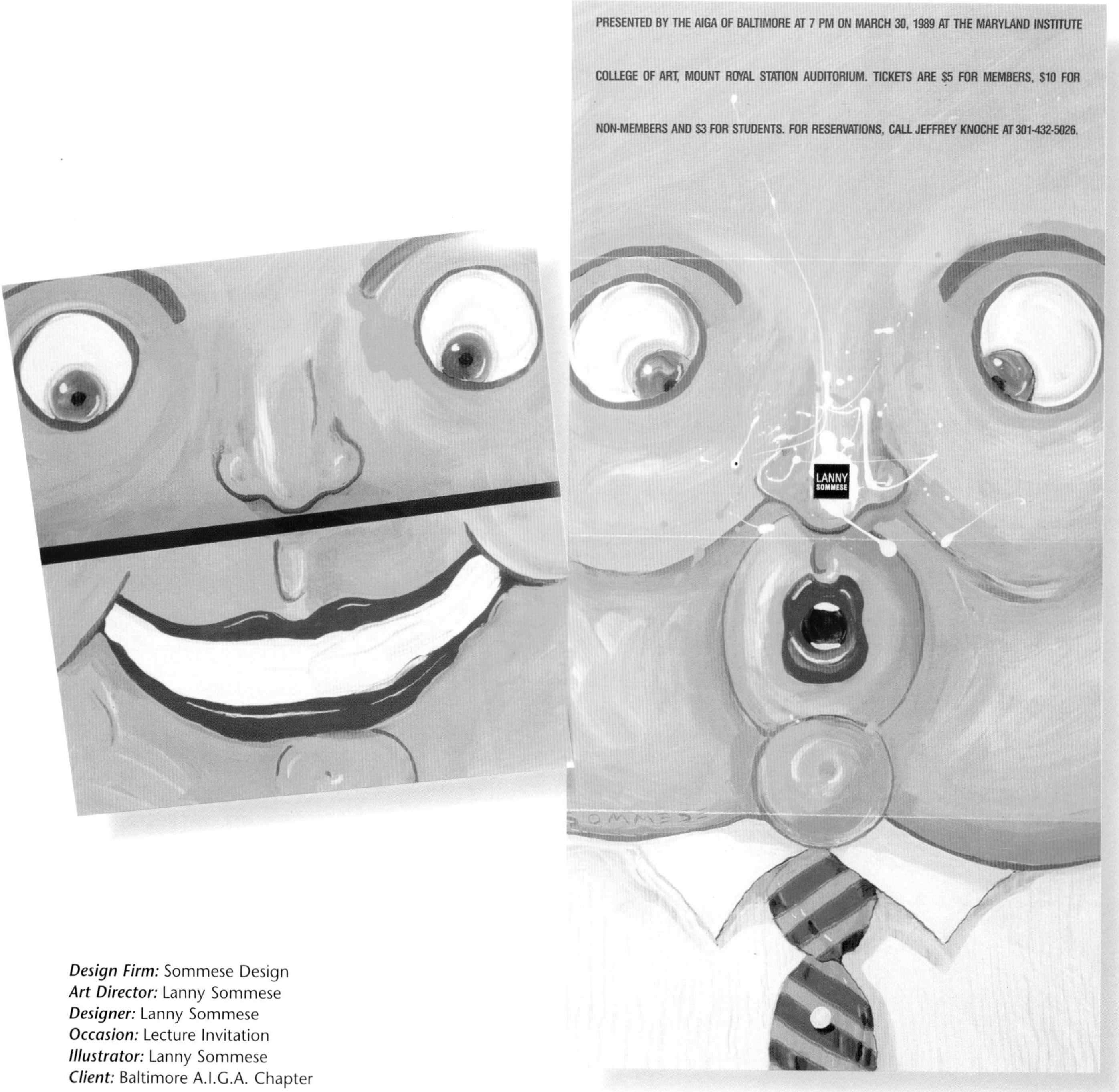

PRESENTED BY THE AIGA OF BALTIMORE AT 7 PM ON MARCH 30, 1989 AT THE MARYLAND INSTITUTE COLLEGE OF ART, MOUNT ROYAL STATION AUDITORIUM. TICKETS ARE $5 FOR MEMBERS, $10 FOR NON-MEMBERS AND $3 FOR STUDENTS. FOR RESERVATIONS, CALL JEFFREY KNOCHE AT 301-432-5026.

Design Firm: Sommese Design
Art Director: Lanny Sommese
Designer: Lanny Sommese
Occasion: Lecture Invitation
Illustrator: Lanny Sommese
Client: Baltimore A.I.G.A. Chapter

46

1

2

1
Design Firm: John Brady Design Consultants
Art Director: John Brady
Designer: Joseph Tomko
Occasion: Designer Dialogue Series
Photographer: Christopher Caffee
Client: AIGA/Pittsburgh

2
Design Firm: Michael Stanard, Inc.
Art Director: Michael Stanard, Inc.
Designer: Marcos Chavez
Occasion: AIGA Show
Client: AIGA

The catalog's style and illustration are consistent, but each edition's cover is different enough so the recipient recognizes they're seeing something new.

It's the details that make these catalogs winners. For example, Starbucks' products were photographed using special lighting to give the effect of morning sun shining through a kitchen window.

There are five different Starbucks catalogs designed each year—one for every season and one for holiday time. The illustrations and photography depict the catalog's seasonal theme.

Client: Starbucks Coffee Company
Design Firm: Hornall Anderson
Design Works, Inc.,
Seattle, Washington
Catalog Team: Jack Anderson,
Julie Tanagi-Lock, Julie Keenan,
Leslie MacInnes, Ellen Elfering
Copywriter:
Pamela Mason Davey
Illustrator:
Julia LaPine
Photographer:
Darrell Peterson

Warm, rich illustrations on Kraft paper have become a trademark of the Starbucks catalog.

Vivid photography enhances products in this furniture catalog. It was circulated to consumers as well as to stores and distributors.

Client: Baronet
Design Firm: PAPRIKA, Montréal, Québec Canada
All Design By: Louis Gagnon
Photographer: Michel Touchette, François Brunelle

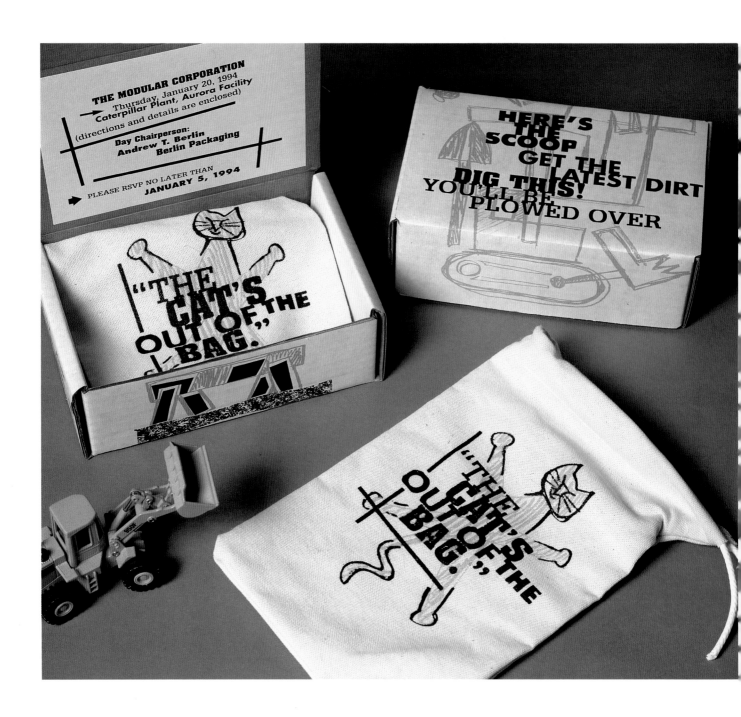

Objective: To creatively invite recipients to attend a program.

Innovation: A toy Caterpillar tractor, representing the product of the event's sponsor, becomes both a keepsake and novel design element when it is placed inside a screen-printed cloth bag and shipped in a corrugated box printed with teaser copy and graphics.

Design Firm: Sayles Graphic Design
Art Director: John Sayles
Designer: John Sayles
Illustrator: John Sayles
Client: Young Presidents Organization

Objective: To create a corporate holiday card that involved the participation of the children of the client's employees.

Innovation: Instead of relying on traditional visuals, the card design takes on the challenge of transforming youngsters' unwieldy scrawls into works of art. Children's drawings were chosen from a client holiday art contest. Interesting folds and simple text animate the piece and direct the focus to the colorful illustrations.

Design Firm: SullivanPerkins
Art Director: Ron Sullivan
Designer: Rob Wilson
Illustrators: Rob Wilson, children of client employees
Client: The Rouse Company

51

1

**Kleine Gesten, große Wirkung.
Geschenke für Ihre Kunden.**

Der Vereinsbank
Geschenkkatalog 1994

Vereinsbank

BAYERISCHE
VEREINSBANK AG

2

1 A catalog of gift ideas for bank customers is sent to branch managers.

Client: Vereinsbank
Design Firm: Gottschalk + Ash International, Zürich, Switzerland
Designer: Thomas Strub, Wolfgang Meder
Photographer: Heiner Bayer

2 Appropriate design details and evocative copy enhance the Laura Ashley image. The development of a design grid makes the overall production process easier. The result? A 30 percent increase in catalog sales.

Client: Laura Ashley, Inc.
Design Firm: Clifford Selbert Design, Cambridge, Massachusetts
All Design By: Nancy Brown, Julia Daggett

In this catalog, the graceful, elegant lines of the eyeOTA product are represented by the movement and expressions of the human body. Models were chosen for their training in yoga and dance.

Design Firm: Wilshire Designs
Art Director: David Kilvert
Designer: Krista Kilvert, David Kilvert
Photographer: Amedeo

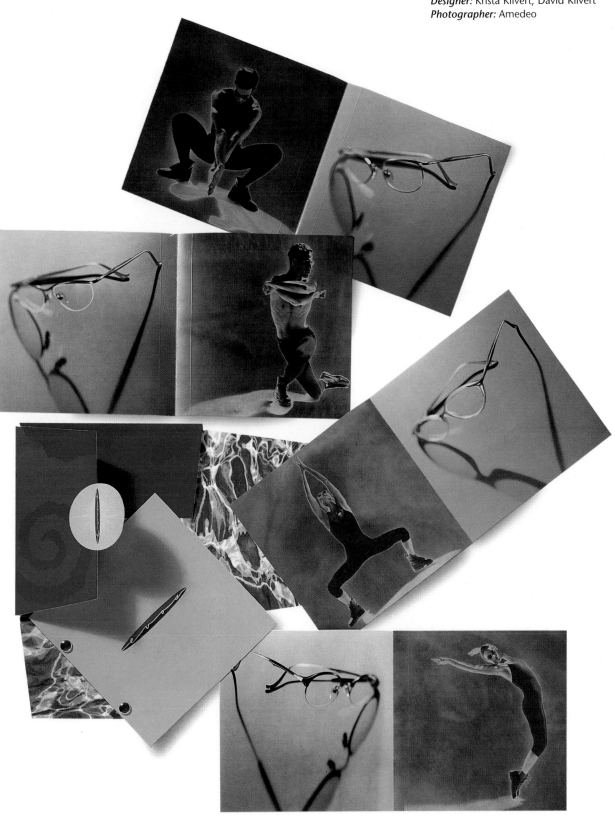

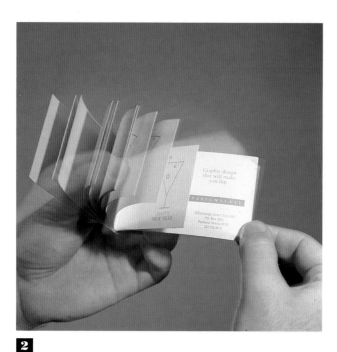

1 This self-promotion artfully packages a variety of logo jobs. The distinctive outer mailer echoes the simplicity of its contents yet is eye-catching enough to catch a recipient's attention. "This promotional package put us on the map and helped me establish my business," says firm principal Carlos Segura.

Design Firm: Segura Inc.
Art Director/Designer: Carlos Segura
Illustrator: Carlos Segura
Client: Segura Inc.

2 Sent to clients and prospects as a holiday greeting, this animated, hand-assembled flip book shows the metamorphasis of a simple line sketch of a Christmas tree (at the opening) into a New Year's champagne glass (at the end). "People kept it," says designer Dan Howard. "It keeps our name in front of our clients."

Design Firm: Designsense
Designer: Dan Howard
Client: Designsense

The 1993 How Design Conference on Business and The Creative Process.

cre**ative v**ision

April 25th thru 28th, 1993. The Westin Hotel, Chicago, Illinois.

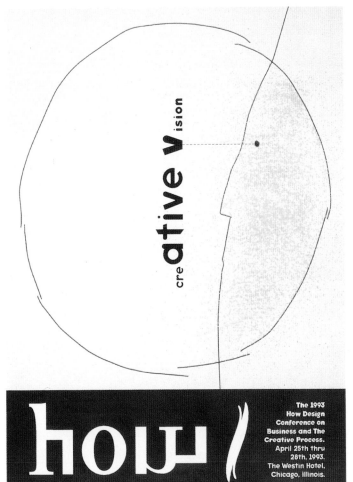

cre**ative v**ision

The 1993 How Design Conference on Business and The Creative Process. April 25th thru 28th, 1993. The Westin Hotel, Chicago, Illinois.

Creating a promotional campaign for a demanding, design-savvy audience, such as *HOW* magazine's readership, can be a formidable task. This series of postcards promoting *HOW*'s Design Conference stimulated a conference discussion on its unusual graphics (used on other conference materials as well). The postcards also achieved results. "That conference was their most successful one to date," says Segura.

Design Firm: Segura Inc.
Art Director/Designer: Carlos Segura
Client: HOW

Design Firm: Siebert Design Associates
Art Director: Lori Siebert
Designer: Lori Siebert, Barb Raymond
Occasion: Trade Show Exhibit
Illustrator: Lori Siebert
Client: Hewlett Packard

1993

Dear Friend of Northlight Theatre,

*B*y definition, North means "situated toward or at the north."
Light is defined as "stimulating vision, enlightening, informative" and Theatre is
"a forum for artistic expression through live performance."

A Friend is described as "one attached to another by affection" and "one who favors
or promotes something." By subscribing to Northlight, you have demonstrated your support
and affection for a theatre that stimulates vision, enlightens, and informs.

*A*s a not-for-profit theatre, Northlight relies on contributions to fulfill
the 40% of the operating budget not covered by ticket sales. We hope that you will show an
additional commitment to Northlight by making a donation to our eighteenth season.

*W*ithout the generosity of individuals like you, Northlight Theatre
would not be possible. Our future is your gift.

*W*ith every good wish,

Russell Vandenbroucke

RUSSELL VANDENBROUCKE
ARTISTIC DIRECTOR, NORTHLIGHT THEATRE

Design Firm: Michael Stanard, Inc.
Art Director: Michael Stanard, Inc.
Designer: Marc Fuhrman
Occasion: Annual Gala Event
Client: Northlight Theatre

Client: Wichita Collegiate School
Design Firm: Love Packaging Group,
Wichita, Kansas
All Design By: Brian Miller

Inside the mailer, a "football field" printed on corrugated slips out of an inner pocket.

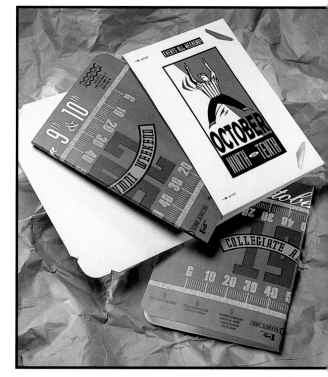

The Collegiate Alumni Weekend mailing was a successful combination of structural and graphic design.

When the recipient opened the "field" a corrugated football literally popped up and out of the mailing.

Since Love Packaging is a corrugated box manufacturer, they had the materials on hand. Love's structural designer, Daryl Hearne, took the original idea, extended the diamond into a football shape and devised internal corrugated hooks that would hold a high tension rubber band—which made the football pop up from a flattened shape.

This two-color brochure promotes a student conference. The brochure was mailed in a die-cut chipboard wrap.

Client: Western Regional Greek Conference
Design Firm: Sayles Graphic Design, Des Moines, Iowa
All Design By: John Sayles

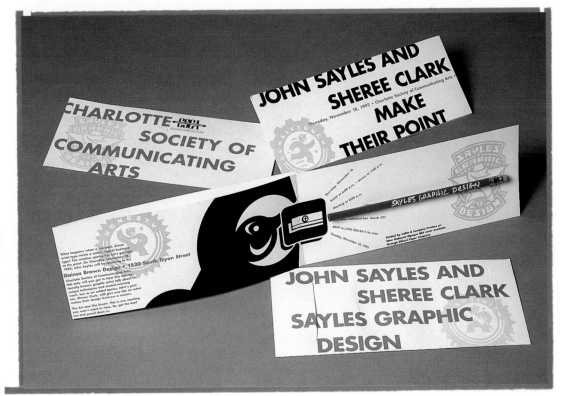

This two-color announcement invites members to hear the speakers "make their point." A pencil was included in the mailing!

Client: Charlotte Society of Communicating Arts
Design Firm: Sayles Graphic Design, Des Moines, Iowa
All Design By: John Sayles

Design Firm: Richard Endly Design, Inc.
Art Director: Bob Berken
Designer: Keith Wolf
Client: Business Incentives, Motorola
Tools: Adobe Illustrator, Adobe Photoshop,
and QuarkXPress

...he designers merged nature with technology,
...owers with fiber optics to create this piece.

Designer: Richard Endly Design, Inc.
Art Director: Lydia Anderson
Designers: Richard Endly and Keith Wolf
Illustrator: Keith Wolf
Client: Business Incentives, AT&T
Tools: QuarkXPress, Adobe Illustrator,
and Adobe Photoshop

This project included a "Call for Art" directed to artists and a subsequent invitation to the Mental Health Association Art Auction. Along with the event information are instructions to bring the invitation to the auction for use as a "bidding paddle."

Client:
Mental Health Association
Design Firm:
Love Packaging Group, Wichita, Kansas
Art Director: Tracy Holdeman
Designer: Brian Miller, Tracy Holdeman
Illustrator: Tracy Holdeman, Brian Miller

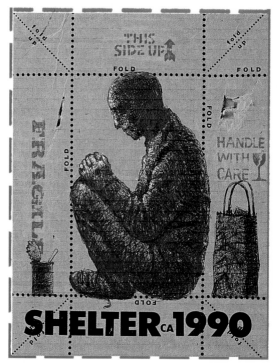

Part of a series, this postcard reflects the "shelter" theme adopted by the non-profit group. The original art for the postcard was created on corrugated cardboard using permanent markers, then photographed.

Client: Architects, Designers and Planners for Social Responsibility
Design Firm: Kiyoshi Kanai Inc. New York, New York
All Design By: Kiyoshi Kanai

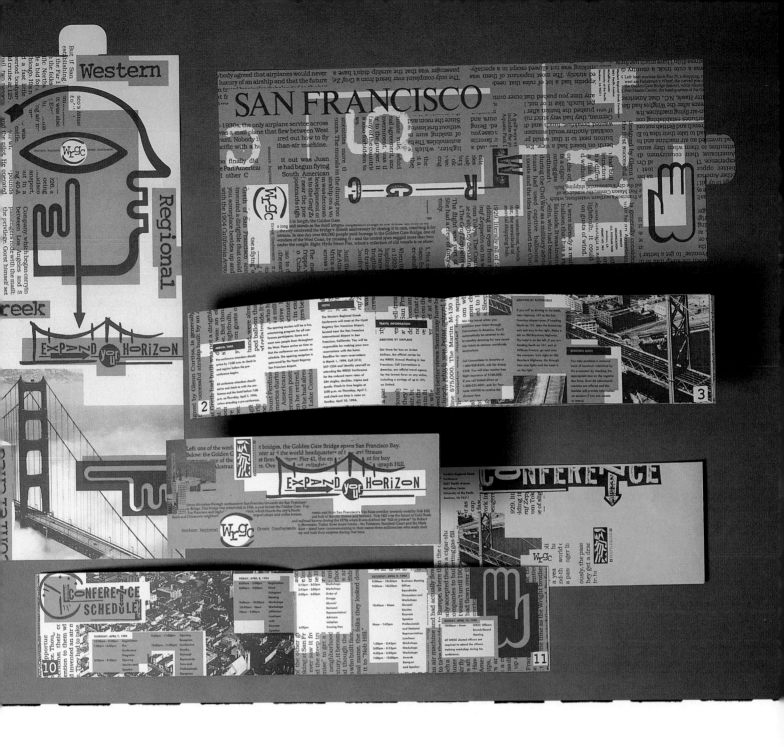

Illustrations of bridges and a vertical format complete
the theme of this brochure, "Expand Your Horizon."

Client: Western Regional Greek Conference
Design Firm: Sayles Graphic Design, Des Moines, Iowa
All Design By: John Sayles

Client: American Players Theatre
Design Firm: Planet Design Company,
Madison, Wisconsin
Art Directors: Dana Lytle, Kevin Wade
Designers: Dana Lytle, Martha Graettinger
Copywriter: John Anderson
Photographer: Taliesin Architects, Mike Rebholz

The brochure was targeted to 10 potential major donors to the theatre's retractable canopy fund-raising campaign. The architect's drawing was included to clearly demonstrate the mechanics of the project.

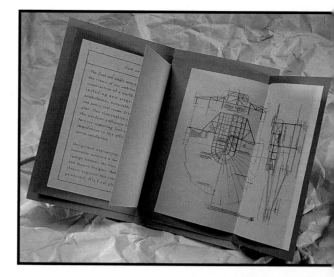

The recipient removes a slipband from the book in order to get inside.

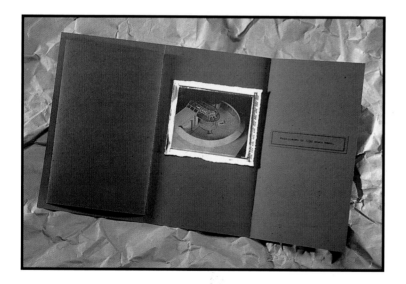

The finished product resembles a hand-bound, limited-edition book. It reflects the one-of-a-kind uniqueness of the theatre and the retractable canopy fund-raising project.

The brochures were created to be produced by the design firm in-house. Typesetting was done on a computer, and the brochures were reproduced by photocopying. The photograph of the model was accomplished by using a Polaroid-transfer process.

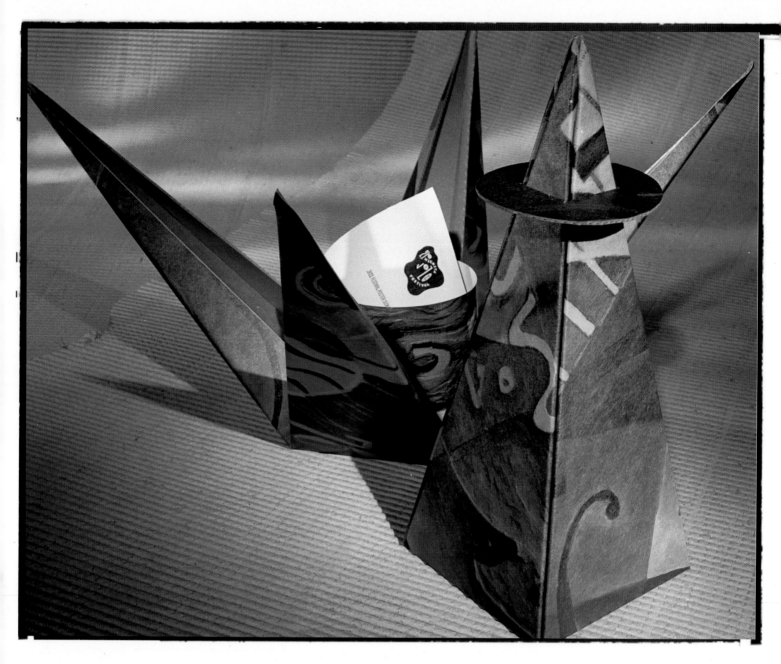

This elaborate invitation falls open when the closure disk is lifted. Inside a rolled sheet contains details.

Client: Wichita Jazz Festival
Design Firm: Love Packaging Group, Wichita, Kansas
All Design By: Tracy Holdeman
Photographer: Rock Island Studios

IF YOU CAN TAKE THAT EVERY DAY, WHAT'S ONE MORE NIGHT?

Design Firm: After Hours Creative
Art Director: Russ Haan
Designer: Sharp Emmons
Client: Phoenix Advertising Club

Objective: To invite firms to submit work for an advertising competition.

Innovation: It is not customary to shoot holes in the pieces you create. In this case, the studio simulated "target practice" by actually hand-drilling hundreds of perforations to make the materials look as if they survived a session on a firearms range.

Design Firm: Samenwerkende Ontwerpers
Art Director: André Toet
Designer: Helene Skjelten
Illustrator: Bart van Leeuwen
Client: ISTD Fine Paper Ltd.

Objective: To design an invitation for a brunch celebrating the launch of a new paper.

Innovation: Here's an invitation that pokes fun at the guests as well as the event. Cartoons illustrate images of the well-known designers invited, whose speech balloons maintain a supposedly unenthusiastic reaction about the upcoming brunch: "I'm not going" or "I'm not wasting my time there"—which, of course, ensured the event was packed.

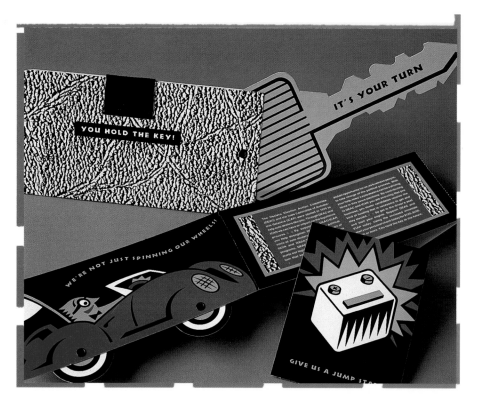

To raise money for its political action committee, an association of auto dealers sent a die-cut mailer proclaiming "You Hold the Key!" A follow-up postcard urges donors to "Give us a jump start."

Client: Iowa Association of Auto Dealers
Design Firm: Sayles Graphic Design, Des Moines, Iowa
All Design By: John Sayles

The outside of the mailer tells the recipient "The wrong legislation could be a bitter pill to swallow." Inside, a vial of Sweet Tart candies completes the concept.

Client: Iowa Medical Society
Design Firm: Sayles Graphic Design, Des Moines, Iowa
All Design By: John Sayles

This memorable and cost-effective Halloween promotion included a real bulb of garlic.

Client: John Brady Design Consultants
Design Firm: John Brady Design Consultants, Pittsburgh, Pennsylvania
Art Director: John Brady
Designer: Gina Kennedy

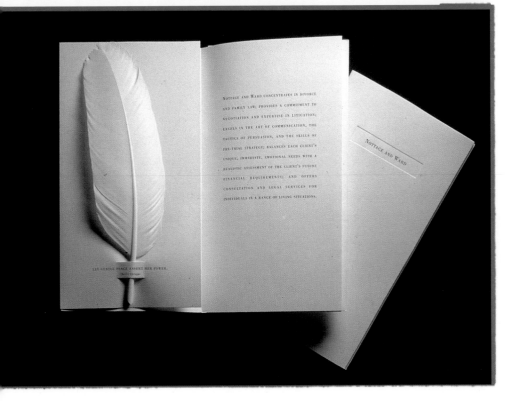

Client: Nottage and Ward
Design Firm: Concrete, Chicago, Illinois
Designer: Jilly Simons, David Robeson
Photographer: Francois Robert

This announcement for a legal practice, entitled "Gentle Peace," is successful because its judicious use of language, imagery, and materials communicates the firm's sensitivity to the individual needs of its clients.

Objective: To design a thank-you card for paper specifiers.

Innovation: An unexpected bouquet of flowers blooms from a folded paper cone, with a laser-cut card heralding the thoughtful message.

Design Firm: Trickett & Webb
Art Directors: Brian Webb, Lynn Trickett, Martin Cox
Designer: Martin Cox
Illustrators: Trickett & Webb
Client: ISTD Fine Paper Ltd.

Menomonee

This was a pro-bono project for the Boys Club of Chicago. The illustration was donated; the printing was 1-color and manually collated.

Design Firm: Segura, Inc.
Designer: Carlos Segura
Art Director: Carlos Segura
Illustrator: Mary Flook Lempa

Client: Tom Fowler, Inc.
Design Firm: Tom Fowler, Inc.
Stamford, Connecticut
All Design By: Thomas G. Fowler

This invitation arrives wrapped in a brown corrugated cardboard sleeve. The words "tic tic tic" are repeated around the sleeve to get the viewer to open up the package to see what is "ticking." The recipient soon realizes the box itself is a clock and an invitation to a holiday party.

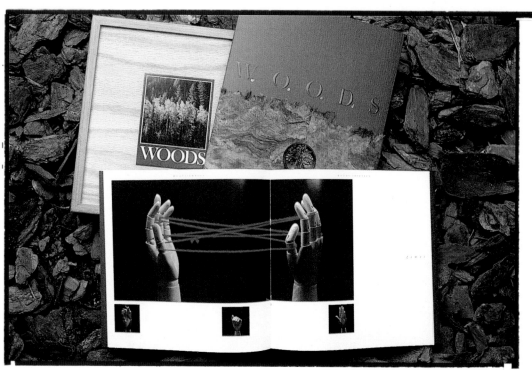

Wrapped in a band of handmade paper, this brochure is nested in a custom, wooden box.

Client: H.T. Woods
Design Firm: Tom Fowler, Inc.,
Stamford, Connecticut
Art Director: Thomas G. Fowler
Designer: Thomas G. Flower,
Karl S. Maruyamam
Photographer: Randy Duchaine

Once unfolded, this unusual invitation expands to over forty inches. It is wrapped in a custom, corrugated cardboard sleeve with a colorful graphic seal establishing the look for the inside panels.

Client: Tom Fowler, Inc.
Design Firm: Tom Fowler, Inc., Stamford, Connecticut
All Design By: Thomas G. Fowler

Arriving flat in a 6" x 9" envelope, this invitation folds into a paper replica of the awards to be given at the ceremony. Event information is printed on the sides of the cube.

Client:
The Art Directors Club
Art Director:
Jean Govoni, Sag Harbor, New York
Designer: Jean Govoni
Photographer: Ted Morrison, Halley Ganges

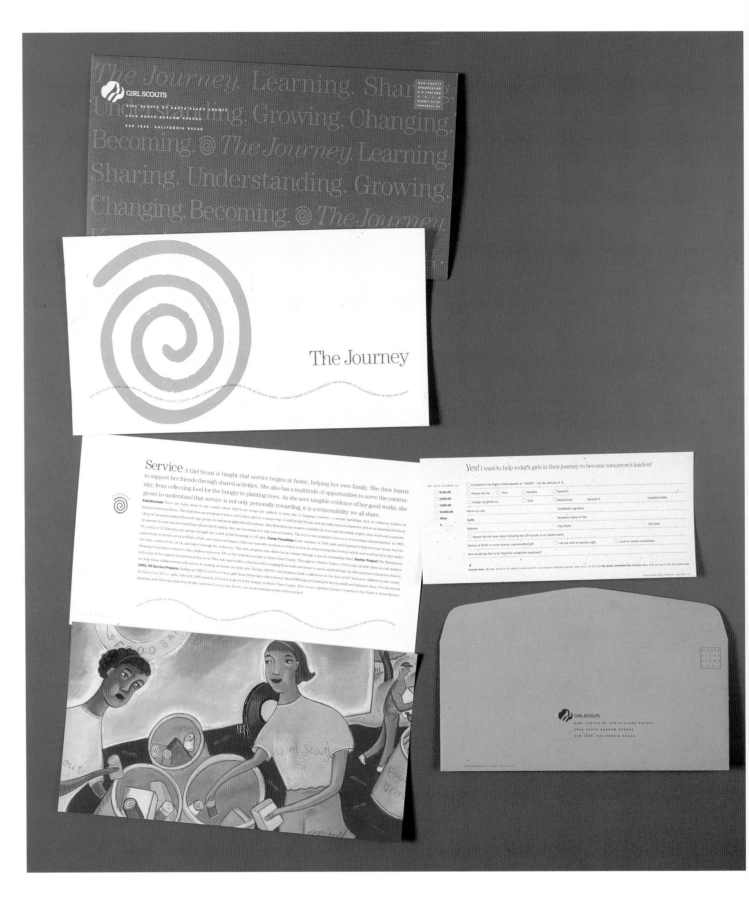

The objective of this annual report is to elevate awareness of the Girl Scouts and their philosophies. The overall design, unique size, and mailing sleeve emphasize the ongoing message "The Journey." In essence, the theme becomes the package.

Design Firm: Melissa Passehl Design
Art Director: Melissa Passehl
Designer: Melissa Passehl
Illustrator: Mercedes McDonald
Copywriter: Susan Sharpe
Client: Girl Scouts of Santa Clara County
Paper/Printer: Simpson, Potlatch, Kirk, Hatcher Trade Press, Meitzler Printing

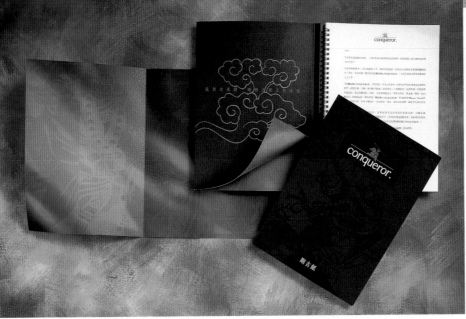

The brochure describes the company's products and capabilities using the theme of "The Liangshan Heroes"—an ancient Chinese legend about warriors who brought unruly times to order. The piece aims to educate its market about the standardization of paper sizes in a confused and non-standard printing environment. Actual paper and printing samples demonstrate the company's ability to conquer even the most challenging high-tech printing effects.

Design Firm: Artailor Design House
Art Director: Raymond Lam
Designer: Raymond Lam
Photographer: Dynasty Commercial Photography
Client: Enpa Company Limited
Paper/Printer: Conqueror

Design Firm: Mires Design
Art Director: Jose Serrano
Designer: Jose Serrano and Mike Brower
Photographer: Carl Vanderschult
Client: Ektelon

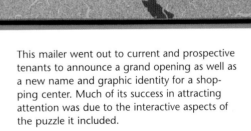

This mailer went out to current and prospective tenants to announce a grand opening as well as a new name and graphic identity for a shopping center. Much of its success in attracting attention was due to the interactive aspects of the puzzle it included.

Design Firm: Hornall Anderson Design Works
Art Director: Jack Anderson
Designer: Jack Anderson, Cliff Chung,
David Bates
Illustrator: Bruce Hale
Calligrapher: David Bates
Client: Northwest Building Corporation

Vote

This promotional mailer was printed on recycled
Simpson Evergreen Birch paper.

Design Firm: Mires Design, Inc.
Art Director: John Ball
Designer: John Ball
Illustrator: David Quattrociocchi
Client: Communicating Arts Group
Printer: Graphics Ink

What does it mean to be

...ive? The modern definition

...esn't require world records

...r perfect form. It's about

...chronizing mind and body,

...ushing performance levels,

...ring new ground, and always

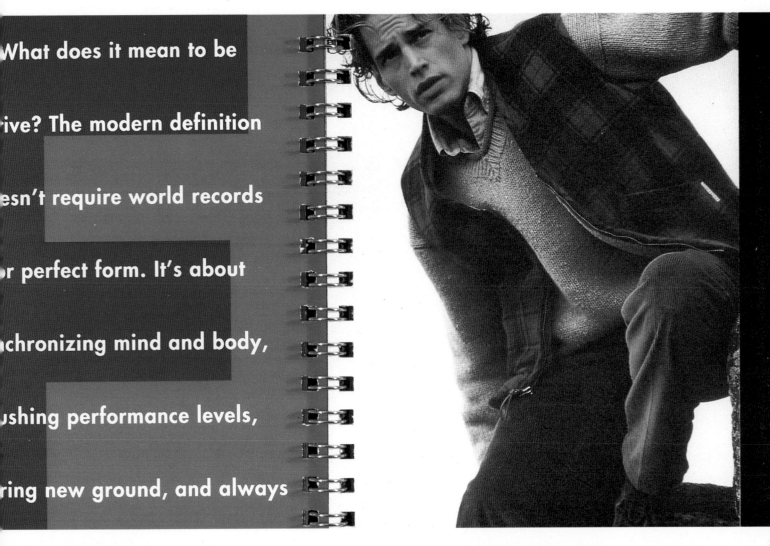

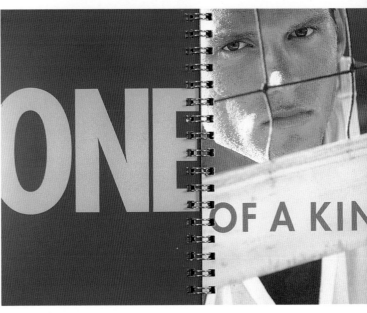

ONE
OF A KIN...

This is a teaser: as the first piece of communica-ions sent to buyers and the press to introduce he Filasport collection, the brochure had to be eye-catching, emotional, and memorable. It also has to introduce an Italian brand to the American market.

Design Firm: Desgrippes Gobé & Associates
Art Director: William Hovard
Photographer: Guzman
Copywriters: Tara Kasaks and Leslie Sherr
Client: Filasport USA

Direct mail can by wildly successful, or a waste of corporate resources. The designer's hand weighs heavily in the success or failure of a direct-mail campaign. This book gives designers an inside look at how world-class design firms make their work stand out in the mountain of mail we receive every day.

Showing the best artwork taken from Rockport Publishers' archives, the Design Library provides professionals, amateurs, and students with a complete, affordable set of design books that will inspire new designs for years to come.

Other titles in the Design Library include:

Brochure

T-Shirt

Illustration

Music

Packaging

Promotion

Logo & Letterhead

Airbrush

Business Card

Poster

Restaurant & Retail

Digital Graphics

$14.99

ISBN 1-56496-337-3

9 781564 963376

90000